The Journey

A SEASON OF REFLECTIONS

The Journey: Walking the Road to Bethlehem

Book
The Journey
Travel the road to Jesus' birth.
978-1-426-71425-2

Reflections
The Journey: A Season of Reflections
Four weeks of reflection on the road.
978-1-426-71426-9

DVD
The Journey: DVD with Leader Guide
Walk with Adam Hamilton in the Holy Land.
978-1-426-71999-8

Individual videos are available for online viewing at the Web address below.

For more information, visit www.JourneyThisChristmas.com.

Also by Adam Hamilton

24 Hours That Changed the World
Why? Making Sense of God's Will
When Christians Get It Wrong
Enough
Seeing Gray in a World of Black and White
Christianity's Family Tree

Selling Swimsuits in the Arctic
Christianity and World Religions
Confronting the Controversies
Making Love Last a Lifetime
Unleashing the Word
Leading Beyond the Walls

ADAM HAMILTON

The Journey

A SEASON OF REFLECTIONS

Abingdon Press
Nashville

The Journey:
A Season of Reflections
by Adam Hamilton

Copyright © 2011 by Abingdon Press.

Scripture quotations in this publication, unless otherwise indicated, are from the New Revised Standard Version of the Bible, copyright 1989, Division of Christian Education of the National Council of the Churches of Christ in the United States of America. Used by permission. All rights reserved.

Scripture quotations marked KJV are from the King James or Authorized Version of the Bible.

Scripture quotations marked CEB are from the Common English Bible, © Copyright 2010 by Common English Bible, and are used by permission.

This book is printed on acid-free, elemental chlorine-free paper.

ISBN: 978-1-426-71426-9

11 12 13 14 15 16 17 18 19 20—10 9 8 7 6 5 4 3 2
MANUFACTURED IN THE UNITED STATES OF AMERICA.

Contents

Introduction

IT'S SNOWING OUTSIDE. I'm sitting in front of the fireplace, computer on my lap, Bible at my side, beginning to write four weeks of reflections to go with my book, *The Journey: Walking the Road to Bethlehem*. That book, designed for personal use or group study, takes an in-depth look at the stories surrounding Jesus' birth, as found in the Gospels of Matthew and Luke. It includes historical information helpful to understanding the Christmas story, as well as firsthand descriptions of the places where the stories took place and thoughts about the meaning of the stories.

There are also videos that go along with *The Journey*. In them, I walk the roads of the Holy Land, taking viewers to the places where the stories occurred. We visit the traditional sites such as Mary's home in Nazareth, Elizabeth's home in Ein Karem, and the Cave of the Nativity in Bethlehem.

Since there is a book and a series of videos, you might ask what need there is for a book of reflections. That was the question I asked my editor. His response: "Think of the reflections as a chance to sit down one-on-one with the reader, as if the two of you were having a conversation over a cup of coffee. Share more personal thoughts and feelings from your own life and ministry, always with an eye to how the story relates to our daily lives."

So, that's what you have in your hand. These are meditations on the Christmas story, based upon the more in-depth study of the story that became *The Journey*.

I invite you to take a journey with me, from the peasant village of Nazareth to the little town of Bethlehem. We'll talk together about Mary, Joseph, Elizabeth and Zechariah, the shepherds, and the wise men, always trying to understanding the significance of the child whose birth brought them all together. My hope and prayer is that you come to see this familiar story with fresh eyes and that its message might change your life as it has changed countless others in the years since that holy night so long ago.

Adam Hamilton

A Word About Advent

ON THANKSGIVING EVENING, hundreds of thousands of Kansas Citians make their way to one of the city's historic shopping districts, the Country Club Plaza. They come to watch as the switch is thrown on the 280,000 colored lights that adorn the buildings. This event has been a Kansas City tradition for over eighty years. When I was growing up, it marked the official beginning of the Christmas season.

Today, radio stations and shopping centers begin playing Christmas music weeks before Thanksgiving. Halloween now seems to be the unofficial beginning of the Christmas season! Yet somehow, though we've extended the season of Christmas, we have moved further and further from the meaning of Christmas.

Christmas today seems like an orgy of overindulgence. Many Americans go into debt to make sure their children have "enough" under the tree at Christmas and then watch as their kids become weary after opening so many presents. We find ourselves with a "Christmas hangover" when the credit card bills arrive. Somehow we miss out on the true message and joy of Christmas.

This is why now, more than ever, Advent matters. Advent is the way the church prepares for Christmas. Since sometime in the late fifth or early sixth century, this season has been a time to recall the meaning of Christmas. The word *Advent* is from the Latin *adventus*, and it means "coming." Christians use this opportunity both to recall Jesus' coming to the earth as a babe in Bethlehem and to prepare themselves for his promised return to earth. The Advent season begins four Sundays before Christmas Day, so it lasts from twenty-two to twenty-eight days, depending upon the day when Christmas falls.

In this book I've written four weeks of daily reflections so that, during the longest Advent, you will have a reading for every day of the season. If you are in a shorter Advent season, you might double up on a couple of these readings, or keep reading them for a few days after Christmas.

In a world where so much focus at Christmas is placed on gift giving, card sending, and party attending, the season of Advent itself is a precious gift. Its purpose is to help us remember the story of a peasant girl who gave birth in a stable to a child whose life, death, and resurrection would change the world.

1. The Genealogy of Jesus

Matthew 1:1-17

An account of the genealogy of Jesus the Messiah, the son of David, the son of Abraham. Abraham was the father of Isaac, and Isaac the father of Jacob, and Jacob the father of Judah and his brothers, and Judah the father of Perez and Zerah by Tamar, and Perez the father of Hezron, and Hezron the father of Aram, and Aram the father of Aminadab, and Aminadab the father of Nahshon, and Nahshon the father of Salmon, and Salmon the father of Boaz by Rahab, and Boaz the father of Obed by Ruth, and Obed the father of Jesse, and Jesse the father of King David. And David was the father of Solomon by the wife of Uriah. . . .

My GREAT AUNT, Celia Belle Yoder, keeps our family history. She's ninety-five years old but sharp as a tack and shows no sign of slowing down. I went to visit her a few weeks ago. We spent an hour together as she walked me through our family genealogy. She's a member of the Daughters of the American Revolution, and she can trace our family history back at least four hundred years. She tells me of well-known circuit-riding preachers who started churches a hundred fifty years ago, about Civil War soldiers, and about pioneers on the Oklahoma prairie. She wants me to know who I am and where I came from.

We begin this book of reflections about the stories surrounding the birth of Jesus precisely where Matthew begins the story—with the genealogy of Jesus. Scholars agree that Matthew does not give us a complete genealogy. He gives us just the highlights that he thinks are important. I've included only a portion of the genealogy above, but I would encourage you to read all seventeen verses. Most people just skim them when reading Matthew, but there are important things to notice.

Here are a few of them: First, Matthew's genealogy is a summary of nearly the entire Old Testament, from Genesis 11 to Malachi 4, capturing the stories of the patriarchs, the Israelites' slavery in Egypt, and the exodus from Egypt to the Promised Land; there is David and Solomon and the divided kingdom, the destruction of Israel and the exile of Judah, and finally the return from exile. Here's the point: Jesus' birth is the climax of this entire story of God's relationship with Israel. Jesus is the end to which the entire biblical story was moving.

It is also often rightly noted that Matthew's account of Jesus' genealogy is nearly unique in that it includes five women. Putting women in a genealogy was not unheard of in the first century, but it was unusual. Who are these women, and what do they tell us about Jesus?

Tamar, the mother of Perez, played the role of a prostitute in order to have children after her husband died. Rahab, listed as the mother of Boaz, was a prostitute when she first entered the biblical story. She was also a foreigner. Then there was Ruth, who, like Tamar, was a widow and, like Rahab, was a foreigner. Bathsheba is mentioned next. She was the wife of Uriah the Hittite, which means that she may have been a foreigner, and she was an adulteress (or the victim of rape) at the hands of King David, after which David had her husband killed. She too was a widow. The last of the women mentioned in the genealogy is Mary, a peasant girl whose life we will examine in greater detail in the next reflection.

When my Aunt Celia Belle tells me our family's history, she describes pioneers, soldiers, and preachers. When Matthew tells Jesus' genealogy he lists two prostitutes and an adulteress, women who were outsiders.

Matthew is, in this genealogy, pointing us toward Jesus' identity and mission. Jesus would bring hope to the widow, mercy to the sinner, and good news not just for the Jews, but for all humankind.

Lord, thank you for your love of those whom others see as second class. Thank you for showing mercy to the sinner and compassion to the brokenhearted. As I begin this season of Advent, help me to see you more clearly in the stories surrounding your birth. Amen.

2. A Town in Galilee Called Nazareth

Luke 1:-27

In the sixth month the angel Gabriel was sent by God to a town in Galilee called Nazareth, to a virgin engaged to a man whose name was Joseph, of the house of David. The virgin's name was Mary.

IT WAS "THE OTHER SIDE OF THE TRACKS," if there had been tracks in first-century Palestine. Nazareth was only four miles from the thriving city of Sepphoris with its luxury villas, markets, temples, and Roman theater. You can still walk among the amazing ruins at Sepphoris (Zippori) to this day. You can see Sepphoris from Nazareth, and by car it's only a ten-minute drive; but in Mary's day it was an hour's walk to Sepphoris from Nazareth. Sepphoris was where the "haves" lived. Nazareth was for the "have nots."

Nazareth doesn't even show up on first-century lists of villages in Galilee. It was considered by the Jewish population of the region as insignificant, or worse. In John 1:46, Nathaniel asked, when told that Jesus was from Nazareth, "Can anything good come out of Nazareth?"

A woman, who grew up in poverty, once described for me the formative years of her childhood. She lived in a trailer park at the lower end of the socioeconomic scale. Children teased her at school, calling her "trailer trash," a name they had learned from their parents. Forty years and a law degree later, she was describing how it felt as a child to be made to feel small and insignificant.

When I think of Nazareth I think of her story. If the tradition is correct, Mary's family lived in the cheapest form of affordable housing at that time: a cave.[1] Mary's village was considered of "no account." But it was precisely here that God came looking for a young woman to bear his Son.

God routinely chooses the humble and the least expected in and through whom he might do his greatest work. Mary recognized this in Luke 1:46-55, when she praised God because he "looked with favor on the lowliness of his servant" while he "scattered the proud in the thoughts of their hearts."

Many of us live in Sepphoris. But God's choice of a woman from Nazareth to bear the Christ leads us to see the importance God places on humility; calls us to repent of any ways in which we, like Nathaniel have said, "Can anything good come out of Nazareth?"; and even invites us to reconsider how we celebrate the birth of Jesus.

As you are preparing for Christmas, here's a suggestion: What if this year you recalibrated? What if this year you decided to give away a bit more to people in need and spend a bit less on yourself and your immediate family?

Our family made a commitment several years ago to donate to organizations serving the poor and those in need an amount equal to the total of what we spend on our family and friends at Christmas. This decision forces us to reduce what we spend on people who don't really need anything, so that we can give to those who truly stand in need. In the process, we've found greater joy in our Christmas celebration.[2]

Lord, forgive me for any time I've ever made others feel small. Forgive me for thinking more highly of myself than I ought. And help me, in the words of Paul, to "consider others better than myself." Help me, this Christmas, to look for ways of increasing what I give to those in need. Amen.

---

1. The cave may have included an upper level, as there are steps leading from it. You can see the cave that tradition claims was Mary's home in session 1 of the videos.
2. The idea of giving an amount equal to what we spend on our family came from my friend, Pastor Mike Slaughter, who expands upon this idea in his book *Christmas Is Not Your Birthday* (Abingdon Press, 2011).

3. An Angel Named Gabriel
Luke 1:26-29

In the sixth month the angel Gabriel was sent by God to a town in Galilee called Nazareth, to a virgin engaged to a man whose name was Joseph, of the house of David. The virgin's name was Mary. And he came to her and said, "Greetings, favored one! The Lord is with you." But she was much perplexed by his words and pondered what sort of greeting this might be.

WHAT DO YOU THINK ABOUT ANGELS? A *Washington Times* poll found that half of all Americans believe in them.[1] The other half were not so sure. If we're talking about little babies with wings flitting about shooting arrows into the hearts of lovers, I'm not biting. If we're thinking John Travolta with giant wings as he portrayed the archangel

Michael in a 1996 film, I'm still saying, "Nope." Clarence talking poor George Bailey off the bridge in *It's a Wonderful Life* starts to get a little closer to the angels of the Scriptures, but skip the part about him earning his wings.

When we read about angels in Scripture, it is important to remember that the word *angel* simply means "messenger." Angels typically appear simply as people— no wings, just people. Sometimes their attire is majestic or glorious, but usually they're just strangers with a word from God. Sometimes they come in visions. But sometimes they come in the flesh. The writer of Hebrews notes that some Christians in his day, as they welcomed strangers, had welcomed angels without knowing it.

In our Scripture, Mary was perplexed by Gabriel's words but not by his appearance; hence he appeared as a stranger who told Mary a word about God's will for her life and who invited her to be open and willing to answer God's call.

To my knowledge I've never met the heavenly kind of angel. But there have been many people whose messages changed my life. When I was fourteen years old, a man named Harold Thorson knocked on my door. He spoke with an electrolarynx (a device that looks like a microphone pressed to the throat, to allow speech for those whose larynx has been removed). He was going door to door in my neighborhood, inviting people to church. Though I did not believe in God I was moved by this man's visit and started attending church, and my life was forever changed. While in college I was selling women's shoes in a department store. Belinda came in to try on shoes, but before she left she also invited my wife and me to visit the Methodist church she attended. We'd been looking for a church. Her invitation, and our visit to her church, led to a call to be a part of renewing The United Methodist Church. How different my life would have been had Harold Thorson not gone visiting door to door or Belinda not listened to the nudge in her heart to invite me to her church.

There have been a thousand more messengers since then. I think of the pastors whose preaching I heard week after week, and how God spoke to me through them. My professors at college and seminary, too. My wife has certainly been a messenger from God for me on countless occasions. And members of the church I serve, such as Nancy, whose persistent invitations led me to visit southern Africa years ago, a visit that would have a profound impact upon my ministry.

Which leads me to a question for you: Do you take the time, do you pay attention to what's happening around you, and do you listen so that you don't miss God's angels when they come speaking to you?

Today many of us are so busy, so preoccupied, or in such a hurry that there is no time to listen to how God may be trying to speak to us. Imagine if Gabriel had approached Mary while she was fetching water and she had said, "I'm sorry, I'm really busy right now. Do you think you could come back later?" Or if she had dismissed him as a crackpot when he tried to tell her about God's plans for her life. And yet this is precisely the response many of us would have in our busy and preoccupied lives today.

God speaks through Scripture, through the still small voice of the Holy Spirit; but God also speaks through people (and occasionally heavenly messengers who look like them). Pay attention! Listen, lest you miss out on God's purposes for your life.

Lord, thank you for the people through whom you have spoken to me. Help me to pay attention and to listen for your voice through those you send. Speak, Lord; your servant is listening. Amen.

---

1. http://www.washingtontimes.com/news/2008/sep/19/half-of-americans-believe-in-angels/ Accessed May 31, 2011.

4. "You Will Conceive and Bear a Son"

Luke 1:31-33

"You will conceive in your womb and bear a son, and you will name him Jesus. He will be great, and will be called the Son of the Most High, and the Lord God will give to him the throne of his ancestor David. He will reign over the house of Jacob forever, and of his kingdom there will be no end."

THE STORIES OF THE ANNUNCIATION and the virgin birth are meant to teach us not primarily about Mary, but about the child she would bear. In our passage today, Gabriel said a great deal about Jesus. You might read it again and underline each word or statement concerning the child Mary would bear. Gabriel was telling Mary she would give birth to the long-awaited messianic king.

A thousand years before Gabriel's conversation with Mary, God sent a messenger to King David. This messenger's name was Nathan, and he was one of God's prophets. Nathan, speaking on behalf of God, said to David, "Your house and your kingdom shall be made sure forever before me; your throne shall be established forever" (2 Samuel 7:16). For four hundred years a descendant of David ruled in Jerusalem.

But in 586 B.C. Jerusalem was destroyed by the Babylonians. The Davidic king, Zedekiah, was arrested by the Babylonians. His sons were executed while he watched, and then his eyes were gouged out and he was led away in chains as a prisoner to Babylon.[1] The leading citizens were exiled to Babylon, others fled to Egypt, and the rest were scattered. For fifty years the Jews remained in exile. During this time the prophets of the Exile reminded the Jewish people of the promise made to David, that his throne would "be established forever." Surely this meant that, despite their current circumstances, there was still hope that God would restore his people.

Thus the people began to hope and pray for God to send an anointed king who once more would rule over God's people. They began to dream about what he would be like and what his kingdom would be like. This was the beginning of the messianic hope. And it was these hopes, dreams, and promises that Gabriel announced would be fulfilled in Jesus, whose name itself means "Deliverer" or "Savior."

Jesus was born to be a king. He was born to rule over a kingdom. When he began his public ministry, he preached, "Repent, for the kingdom of God is at hand" (see Mark 1:15 KJV). His entire ministry was focused on teaching about God's kingdom and inviting his hearers to be a part of it. That kingdom is not some future heavenly realm; it is a reality today. Jesus said, "The kingdom of

God is within you" (Luke 17:21 KJV). Whenever and wherever we choose to follow Jesus and to live as his people, we become citizens of his kingdom.

Jesus said those who are citizens in his kingdom, who follow him as king, will love their neighbors and even their enemies. He said they will feed the hungry, clothe the naked, give drink to the thirsty, visit the sick and imprisoned, and welcome the stranger. How would Jesus have us celebrate his birth? I think he would say, "By doing my will and living the precepts I taught you."

I was struck recently by the actions of a child who understood this. His name is Jake. For his fifth birthday his parents threw him a birthday party. He invited all his friends. But he told his friends the only presents he wanted were jars of peanut butter. Jake had heard there were children in Kansas City who received breakfast and lunch at school each day, but on the weekends there was little food in their homes. They were coming to school hungry on Monday mornings. Our church started a program to send backpacks home with these children every Friday filled with snacks to tide them over for the weekend. Included among those snacks were jars of peanut butter. Jake decided that for his birthday he wanted other children not to be hungry over the weekend.

Jake is learning what it means to call Jesus his king. How might you follow his example this Christmas?

Lord, in this season of Advent, as I read the stories surrounding your birth, I once more acknowledge you as my king. How grateful I am that you reign forever. Help me today, and each day, to live as a citizen of your kingdom. Amen.

---

1. You can read this story in 2 Kings 25.

5. "Here Am I, the Servant of the Lord"

Luke 1:38

Then Mary said, "Here am I, the servant of the Lord; let it be with me according to your word."

IMAGINE THIRTEEN-YEAR-OLD MARY hearing from the messenger that she would have a child, conceived out of wedlock, who would grow up to be the messianic king. Those words would have made it appear, from her vantage point, that the child she was to bear would be a direct threat to both King Herod and the Roman Empire. If the child's identity were found out, then the child, and she, would be killed. Herod had already killed two of his own children, along with his favorite wife, because he believed they dreamed of taking over his throne. Viewed in this light, we can see that the messenger had brought to Mary a dangerous request from God.

But it didn't stop with the obvious danger of giving birth to a son who was to be king. There was also the matter of the child being conceived outside of wedlock. The law commanded that if a woman engaged to be married was found pregnant by another man, she was to be put to death. God's request to Mary was dangerous indeed.

Then there were Mary's hopes and dreams for her own life. She was to marry the carpenter Joseph. But now, how would this work? He would not believe her story—how could he? God's request would mean the end of their engagement. People in her hometown would discover she was pregnant, and she would be considered promiscuous or worse. Add to this the fact that Mary was being asked to give birth, no small request in a day and time before modern medicine. Women died giving birth.

Gabriel, on behalf of God, was asking a great deal of this frightened young girl. William Barclay captures the message of this scene for all of us when he says, "The piercing truth is that God does not choose a person for ease and comfort and selfish joy but for a task that will take all that head and heart and hand can bring to it."[1]

When was the last time you took a risk to pursue what you believed God was calling you to do? When was the last time you did something that made you just a bit afraid because you believed it was the will of God?

Kristin was a senior in college when she felt God calling her to join the Peace Corps and move to Swaziland to help teach children whose parents had died of HIV/AIDS. At the age of twenty-two, she moved to the small African nation and began her work. The job was hard and filled with challenges and not a little danger. But ask her today how she feels about her time in Swaziland, and she'll tell you it was among the greatest blessings of her life.

If God called you to Swaziland, would you go? What about to the heart of your own city? Mary's response to God's dangerous call is one of the most beautiful statements in all the Bible. This young girl simply said, "Here am I, the servant of the Lord; let it be with me according to your word." This is a prayer short enough to memorize and important enough to say again and again.

Lord, I hear of opportunities to serve others, or your call to stand up for what is right, or your invitation to give of myself; yet sometimes I am afraid. Forgive me for allowing fear, or my desire for safety and comfort, to keep me from doing your will. Help me to hear your call and to be willing to step out of my comfort zone in order to do your work. "Here am I, the servant of the Lord; let it be with me according to your word." Amen.

---

1. *The Gospel of Luke, Revised Edition of the Daily Bible Study Series* (Westminster John Knox Press, 1975; p. 14)

6. Little Town of Bethlehem

Micah 5:2 and Matthew 2:6

You, O Bethlehem of Ephrathah,
who are one of the little clans of Judah,
from you shall come forth for me
one who is to rule in Israel,
whose origin is from of old,
from ancient days.

"And you, Bethlehem, in the land of Judah,
are by no means least among the rulers of Judah;
for from you shall come a ruler
who is to shepherd my people Israel."

WE TURN FROM THE STORY of the Annunciation (the announcement that Mary would have a child) to the story of how Joseph came to know that Mary was pregnant. First, we turn to his hometown, the "little town of Bethlehem."

For years I thought that Joseph was likely from Nazareth as Mary was, and that Joseph only went to Bethlehem with Mary as a result of the census that we'll consider shortly. But for reasons I describe in the book that accompanies these reflections,[1] I've come to believe that Joseph's hometown was actually Bethlehem. Matthew's Gospel doesn't mention Nazareth until Jesus is likely several years old, after the return of the Holy Family from Egypt.

Bethlehem was only somewhat larger than Nazareth; but, while Nazareth was considered a town of low esteem ("Can anything good come out of Nazareth?"), men and women would proudly say they hailed from Bethlehem in Judea. The name *Bethlehem* means "House of Bread," probably a nod to the fact that there were farmers, millers, and bakers there who supplied bread for nearby Jerusalem. Bethlehem was best known as the home of

King David and his family. It was known, along with Jerusalem, as "the City of David."

Other well-known people were associated with Bethlehem as well. Jacob buried his beloved wife Rachel near Bethlehem. (The traditional site of her tomb can still be seen outside Bethlehem's wall to this day.) One of the rulers of ancient Israel, Ibzan the judge, was from Bethlehem, and he was also buried there.[2] The Book of Ruth is set in Bethlehem and gives us a glimpse of what the village was like eleven hundred years before the time of Jesus.

All these people were a part of the rich history of Bethlehem. Yet it was the words of the prophet Micah that made Bethlehem a name synonymous with hope and with God's future deliverance of his people. Bethlehem was the name associated with a promise that God would not abandon his people. One day God would send a ruler who would "stand and feed his flock in the strength of the LORD" (Micah 5:4) and who, as king, would "be the one of peace" (Micah 5:5). This promise of a king who would shepherd his people and bring them peace sustained the Jewish people over the centuries. The promise, and Bethlehem as a symbol for it, gave them hope in exile, in war, and in adversity. They believed that one day, from Bethlehem, would come a shepherd king, a man of peace.

Henry Wadsworth Longfellow, the great American poet, wrote a poem on Christmas Day 1864 while the Civil War raged. Three years earlier, his beloved wife Fanny had died. His heart had been broken by her loss, and for some time he was unable to compose verse. But that year he wrote of an undying hope associated with Christmas in a poem originally called "Christmas Bells." In that poem he wrote of the war and the cannons drowning out the sound of "peace on earth, good will to men." But he ended the poem with these words:

And in despair I bowed my head;
"There is no peace on earth," I said;
   "For hate is strong,
   And mocks the song
Of peace on earth, good-will to men!"

Then pealed the bells more loud and deep:
"God is not dead; nor doth He sleep;
   The Wrong shall fail,
   The Right prevail,
With peace on earth, good-will to men!"

Longfellow captured in his poem the effect that Micah's words about Bethlehem had on future generations. When hate seems strong and mocks the song, we remember the words of promise, both from Micah and from the angels at Jesus' birth, that with his birth came the certain promise of "peace on earth, good-will to men."

Lord, during this season of Advent I remember the promise that you would "be the one of peace" and long for the day when peace will reign on earth. Help me to remember and trust that "the wrong shall fail, the right prevail." And make me an instrument of your peace. O come, O come, Emmanuel! Amen.

---

1. The book, *The Journey: Walking the Road to Bethlehem*, contains a more detailed study of the events leading up to and including the birth of Jesus. It includes maps, historical and archaeological details while this book of reflections is focused on offering meditations on the meaning of the Christmas story. The two books are meant to be used hand in hand, alongside the videos mentioned in an earlier reflection that we filmed in the Holy Land at the places these events occurred.
2. Judges 12:8-10, though some believe this Bethlehem was in the north.

7. Joseph the Carpenter
Matthew 13:54-55

[Jesus] came to his hometown and began to teach the people in their synagogue, so that they were astounded and said, "Where did this man get this wisdom and these deeds of power? Is not this the carpenter's son?"

In Matthew 13:54-55 we find Jesus preaching in his hometown. Some of the townsfolk questioned his credibility and ministry. They were not earnestly wondering where he got his wisdom and power; they were attempting to discredit him because he was only a "carpenter's son."

The word used here for carpenter, *tekton*, signifies a common laborer working with his hands, usually in wood, though the word was also at times used to describe stone masons. So Joseph might have been a builder, or a furniture maker, or one who built farm implements. He might also have been a handyman who fixed things for folks. There were carpenters who were master builders: they were called *archtektons* (from which we get our word *architect*); but Joseph was only a *tekton*—an ordinary builder, woodworker, or handyman.

This humble estate of Joseph is consistent with the picture we have of him in the Gospel accounts where he is present. Unlike Mary, Joseph has no "lines"—we don't read a single word he speaks in the Gospels. It is universally recognized that he played an important role in the life of Jesus, but there are no "hail Josephs" offered to him. He is the patron saint of those who serve and do the right thing without seeking any credit.

I sat in a meeting recently in which I received reports about our clothing ministry at the church. As part of the ministry, our members donate clothing in good condition. It is sorted, separated by size and style, and then carefully folded or hung on hangers and delivered to area homeless shelters and programs for low-income people. The workers in these programs love the fact that our volunteers so skillfully and lovingly prepare the clothes for their people. When I asked about these volunteers, I was told that there are twenty people who spend from nine to eleven o'clock three mornings a week doing this work, that they don't want to be recognized, and that they don't look for any credit except what comes from knowing that they are helping people in need. The person telling me this said, "They are a team of twenty Josephs."

Of all the qualities Jesus learned from Joseph, I suspect the most important had to do with humility and servanthood. When Jesus taught his disciples that "whoever wishes to be great among you must be your servant"

(Matthew 20:26), when he washed his disciples' feet at the Last Supper (John 13), and when he said to them, "Those who humble themselves will be exalted" (Luke 14:11), I believe he was teaching what he'd seen modeled by Joseph's life.

Lord, forgive me for those moments when I've sought the limelight or resented others for outshining me. Forgive me for those times when I've forgotten your call to "in humility regard others as better than yourselves."[1] Help me, that I might, like Joseph, live as your humble servant. Amen.

---

1. Philippians 2:3

8. The Doubter?

Matthew 1:18-21

Now the birth of Jesus the Messiah took place in this way. When his mother Mary had been engaged to Joseph, but before they lived together, she was found to be with child from the Holy Spirit. Her husband Joseph, being a righteous man and unwilling to expose her to public disgrace, planned to dismiss her quietly. But just when he had resolved to do this, an angel of the Lord appeared to him in a dream and said, "Joseph, son of David, do not be afraid to take Mary as your wife, for the child conceived in her is from the Holy Spirit. She will bear a son, and you are to name him Jesus, for he will save his people from their sins."

DO YOU EVER STRUGGLE WITH DOUBT? I know some people who seem never to doubt. They tell me that "I know that

I know that I know that I know" that this or that thing is true. But faith has not come quite that easily for me. Over the years I've questioned and studied and wrestled with my faith. Some things I no longer wrestle with—I choose to believe them based upon the witness of Scripture.

Some decry doubt, as though it were the enemy of faith. But doubt is not the enemy of faith; it is often the doorway to a deeper faith.

I take great comfort in the fact that some of the most challenging Christian doctrines to believe, namely the virgin birth and the Resurrection, were difficult even for the people who were first confronted with these ideas.

Let's consider the Resurrection, for example. When the women who first saw the empty tomb told the disciples that Jesus was raised from the dead, the disciples didn't believe. When the disciples saw Jesus raised but Thomas wasn't with them, and they told Thomas, Thomas refused to believe.

In our Scripture today we find Mary telling Joseph that she was pregnant and that the pregnancy was a miracle somehow made possible by the Holy Spirit. Did Joseph believe in the "virginal conception"? Not yet. In fact, he was so convinced she was making up the story that he planned to break off the engagement and have nothing to do with Mary again!

Joseph was the first person in the Gospel who doubted; he might be considered (with "Doubting Thomas") the patron saint of doubters. Yet Joseph, after hearing from God in a dream that Mary was telling the truth, chose to believe her. And that decision changed the course of his life and the life of the child he would raise as his own.

How do you overcome doubt? You remain open to possibilities, as Joseph was. You listen and watch and you weigh the testimony of the Gospels and of modern-day disciples. Belief, in the end, is a choice. You look at the evidence and testimony available to you, and in the end you make a choice. You choose to trust, and to believe.

Lord, help me to be patient when others doubt. Help me, when I share my faith, to be a credible witness. And help me, Lord, to trust in those truths I don't fully understand, but which you know to be true. Amen.

9. Being a Righteous Man...
Matthew 1:18b-19

Mary had been engaged to Joseph, but before they lived together, she was found to be with child from the Holy Spirit. Her husband Joseph, being a righteous man and unwilling to expose her to public disgrace, planned to dismiss her quietly.

WE OFTEN READ MATTHEW'S ACCOUNT of Joseph's "annunciation"—that is, his learning that Mary was going to bear the Christ—without really seeing what was happening here. His fiancée was pregnant. She told him a strange man had come and told her she was going to have a baby and, as far as she knew, she was already pregnant. The man promised her the child would one day be the long-awaited Messiah. If you were Joseph, her fifteen- or sixteen-year-old fiancé, what would you be feeling as Mary told you this? We know that at first Joseph did not believe her story. What did he believe? Do you think he took this news calmly?

I have met with dozens of people in my congregation after they discovered their spouses had been unfaithful. This is painful enough. But in the case of Joseph's discovery, Mary was carrying the baby of the one with whom she had been unfaithful. (Again, keep in mind that Joseph did not yet believe Mary's story about a virginal conception; he believed she had been with another man.)

What words would you use to describe what Joseph must have been feeling? Betrayal? Hurt? Anger? Do you think he was brought to tears when he was all alone, thinking about Mary with another man?

The law of Moses made provisions for such cases: "If there is a young woman, a virgin already engaged to be married, and a man meets her in the town and lies with her, you shall bring both of them to the gate of that town and stone them to death" (Deuteronomy 22:23-24). We don't know how often this sentence was actually carried out, or whether such persons were more often merely publicly disgraced, but the penalty was possible; and such penalties are occasionally still carried out in the Middle East.

Listen again to our Scripture: "Joseph, being a righteous man and unwilling to expose her to public disgrace, planned to dismiss her quietly." Despite his hurt and pain he was unwilling to expose Mary to public disgrace. Why not? Matthew tells us it was because Joseph was a "righteous man."

Righteousness or holiness is often seen as closely linked to obeying the law or following the Scriptures. But in this case, Joseph's righteousness led him to ignore the clear teaching of the law. What does this tell us about the New Testament's definition of righteousness?

Righteousness, as exemplified first by Joseph and then by Jesus, is more about showing mercy and compassion than it is following the law. Here Joseph was acting upon the words of another Scripture, in which God said, "I desire mercy, not sacrifice" (Matthew 9:13).

I wonder if there is anyone who has wronged you, for whom Joseph's story is an invitation for you to show mercy. It may not change the one to whom you show mercy, but it most certainly will change you. Blessed are the merciful.

Lord, you know the grievances I carry in my heart for the wounds others have inflicted upon me. Help me to extend compassion and mercy as Joseph did, and in so doing to find true righteousness. Amen.

10. Joseph's Dreams
Matthew 1:20

Just when he had resolved to do this, an angel of the Lord appeared to him in a dream and said, "Joseph, son of David, do not be afraid to take Mary as your wife, for the child conceived in her is from the Holy Spirit."

IT IS NOT BY ACCIDENT that Matthew tells us that, while Gabriel spoke directly to Mary, Joseph's message came in a dream. We can see a connection between this Joseph and the patriarch Joseph, whose story fills nearly thirteen chapters of Genesis. God spoke to that Joseph in dreams (hence the title of Andrew Lloyd Webber and Tim Rice's musical, *Joseph and the Amazing Technicolor Dreamcoat*), and in a similar way God spoke to Joseph the carpenter in dreams. Matthew looks for these kinds of parallels between the Old Testament and the story of Jesus.

Has God ever spoken to you in a dream? I hardly remember the dreams I have when I sleep. But I frequently have what could be called day dreams. Some might call these visions. In them I sometimes see what could be, what I believe God wants to be. These are ideas that come to me while I'm reading Scripture, or hearing someone else preach, or meeting with my small group, or conversing with others. Often these are dreams that come when seeing places of great need. I carry a little black book with me to write down these dreams when they occur, because I quickly forget them.

I pray over these dreams, meditate upon and then test these dreams to see if they appear to be only my ideas, or if it is possible that God has placed these dreams in my heart. I look to see if they line up with Scripture and our church's purpose; if they are personal, I consider how they line up with my personal mission. I share these dreams with my wife and ask for her thoughts. I share them with the lead staff and lay leaders of the church and with my closest friends. All this is a discernment process that helps me avoid chasing after a whim. Over the years, some of the most meaningful and productive things I've been a part of have started with a dream that I felt was from God.

Your dreams may emerge as you hear other people's dreams. Several years ago Karla, one of our staff at the church, felt compelled to start a worship service for senior adults who had Alzheimer's, dementia, or other forms of memory loss. She announced it to area nursing homes, and they began sending buses of people to the worship service in our chapel.

Karla and her team filled the service with well-known hymns, familiar creeds, the Lord's Prayer, and simple messages that might help people remember who they are. Recently the teachers in our daytime Kindermusik program began bringing the little children to sing for this worship service. The three- and four-year-olds sang, "Jesus loves me! This I know, for the Bible tells me so. Little ones to him belong; they are weak but he is strong." As the children sang the chorus, "Yes, Jesus loves me," voices of people who could not remember their own names joined the children: "Yes, Jesus loves me! Yes, Jesus loves me! Yes, Jesus loves me! The Bible tells me so."

The dream of one woman became the dream of a host of volunteers, and together they did what they felt God was leading them to do. The result was something extraordinary.

God spoke to Joseph in dreams. Joseph's dreams called him to devote the rest of his life to nurturing, mentoring, and protecting Jesus. My dreams from God seldom come at night. They are a sense of calling that well up inside

Are you listening for God to speak to you? And if God speaks, are you willing to obey? Listening for God's dreams, and following them, made all the difference in Joseph's life; and it makes all the difference in our lives as well.

Lord, help me to listen for your dreams for my life, and give me the boldness and courage to pursue them. Speak, Lord; your servant is listening. Amen.

11. He Will Save His People From Their Sins

Matthew 1:21

"She will bear a son, and you are to name him Jesus, for he will save his people from their sins."

BEFORE JESUS WAS EVEN BORN, Joseph was told that his son would be humanity's Savior. Jesus—Joshua, as he would have been called by Mary and Joseph[1]—means "the Lord saves." The messenger told Joseph in a dream to give his son that name, because he would save his people from their sins.

I won't try to discuss here how Jesus saves his people from their sins; I've devoted the better part of another book to that.[2] But let's pause for a moment to think about sin and what it means.

The primary Hebrew and Greek words that are translated into English as *sin* mean "to stray from the path" or "to miss the mark." The same Greek word was used to describe what happened when an archer shot an arrow and it missed its target. Sin is a deviation from God's path or mark, and we are all prone to do this. Consider the classic "seven deadly sins": lust, gluttony, greed, indifference, wrath, envy, and pride.[3] Which of us hasn't wrestled with several of these with some regularity? And when we routinely commit these sins, we find that we experience pain and separation from God and others.

I think of several men over the years who have sat in my office in tears describing the breakup of their marriages over infidelity. Or the man I greet after church who cannot seem to break free of his addiction to alcohol, despite the fact that it cost him his family. I think of several church members, professional and respected people in the community, who ended up in prison over choices they made. I think of a woman who wept as I prepared to give her communion, saying she wasn't sure she was good enough to take it. And I think of my own life, and how many times I've done things I have been ashamed of.

I can't see you, but I think I know something about you. This is what I know: you have a few secrets too. There are things you've said or done or thought that you don't want anyone else to know about, things that make you squirm or cringe or even cry when you think about them. Alongside those things you may have done, or thought of doing, are the things you didn't do that you were meant to do— sins of omission, things God was counting on you to do but which you chose to rationalize away.

Part of the gift of Christmas is the gift of a Savior. Jesus came to save us from our sins. He came to show us the way, the truth, and the life. He came to redeem us, suffer for us, cleanse us, forgive us, and heal us. Paul once wrote it this way: "Wretched man that I am, who can save me?" He went on to answer his own question: "Thanks be to God through Jesus Christ our Lord!" (Romans 7:24-25 paraphrase).

Christmas comes with the promise of salvation from our sins, wrought by the child who was born in Bethlehem.

Lord, thank you for mercy and grace. Forgive me for _____ . [Confess those things that you continue to carry guilt over.] *Thank you for sending Jesus to save and deliver me. Help me, in thought, word, and deed, to live a life that pleases you. Amen.*

---

1. *Jesus* is based on the Greek transliteration of his name. Since Mary and Joseph spoke Aramaic, the angels would have told them to call the child Yeshua or Joshua.
2. *24 Hours That Changed the World* (Abingdon Press, 2009) is focused on the final day of Jesus' life and four different theories of the Atonement.
3. There are variations on this list.

12. "They Will Call Him Emmanuel"

Matthew 1:22-23 CEB

Now all of this took place so that what the Lord had spoken through the prophet would be fulfilled:

> *Look! A virgin will become pregnant and give birth to a son,*
> *And they will call him, Emmanuel.*
> *(Emmanuel means "God with us.")*

As I WRITE, CITIES AND TOWNS along the Mississippi River are either flooding or are braced for flooding as the river reaches historic levels in the South. Thousands of people will lose their homes, farms, and businesses. Some will ask, "Where was God in the midst of these floods?" Or more to the point, "Why did God not act to save us?"

I've tried to answer these and other questions about suffering elsewhere,[1] but here I would just say that suffering, natural disasters, and tragedies are a part of life. Our bodies are susceptible to disease. Human beings misuse their freedom and do harmful things to one another. Earthquakes, tornadoes, and floods seem to be part of the equilibrium that makes life on our planet possible.

It seems that generally God does not directly intervene to suspend the forces of nature—either the macro forces that control weather and the movement of tectonic plates, or the micro forces that can cause sickness. Floods occur, and even the most holy people catch colds and suffer from diseases. Neither does God suspend human freedom. As much as it must pain God to watch what we human beings do to one another, God seems to allow human beings to rebel against his will and do things that bring pain to others.

If God doesn't suspend natural laws for us, what does God do? Isaiah 43:2 gives us an idea. There God says, "When you pass through the waters, I will be with you." David, in the best known of all psalms, says, "Even though I walk through the darkest valley, I fear no evil; for you are with me."[2] Again and again in the Scriptures, God promises not freedom from adversity but freedom from fear, hopelessness, and despair because he is with us.

To some, God's promise to be with us may not seem like much. I disagree. I am grateful for the forces of nature that create the mountains and carve the canyons. I am grateful for the natural laws that somehow bring equilibrium to our atmospheric conditions. I am grateful for human freedom and for the bodies we live in, even if they are, by their nature, susceptible to disease.

I feel I can face all these things, provided I know that God is with me, that he won't leave me or forsake me, and that when this earthly life is over he will welcome me to his eternal realm.

This brings us to our passage today. Here Jesus is called, in Hebrew, Emmanuel.[3] *Emmanuel* means "God with us," as Matthew points out to his Greek-speaking readers. Contained in this word is one of the most powerful ideas in the Christmas story. God has not promised us a life without suffering or a world without pain; he has promised to walk with us through the suffering and the pain. In Jesus, God literally has come to us in flesh and blood, so that we might know that he is with us. He has come to suffer with and for us that we might know he understands what human life is like. At the end of his life he was raised from the dead, to assure us that not even death will have the final word in our lives.

I walked into a hospital room not long ago to visit a man who had just been diagnosed with terminal cancer. His wife sat next to him. I wanted to promise them that if we just prayed hard enough, his cancer would be gone. Sometimes that happens, but in my experience those times are rare. More often, doctors do what they can to prolong life. People who pray, trust in God, and have a church family can find peace on their journey. After listening to this man and his wife describe their feelings and emotions, I said to them, "We're going to pray for a miracle. But we also recognize that miracles are not the norm. What is most important for you to know, and what I came to be a visible reminder of, is that God is with you. He will be with you every moment. He will hold you in his arms, and he has promised that this life is only the preface to the great adventure he has prepared for you. Rest in his arms. Trust that he's with you. Know that God loves you."

What difference does it make? When my daughters were small, there would sometimes be terrible storms in the middle of the night, and, terrified, they would run to our room and wake me up. "Daddy, I'm scared," they would cry. I would make a little bed for them next to ours, and I would sit with them and tell them, "Daddy's right here. You don't have to be afraid." They would fall right to sleep. I hadn't stopped the storm, but they knew that if their father was nearby, they didn't need to be afraid.

Jesus is a flesh-and-blood reminder that God walks with us, suffers with us, loves us, has redeemed us, and offers us eternal life. John Wesley, as he lay dying in his chambers near the New City Road Chapel, put it this way: "Best of all, God is with us."

I can face anything if I know that God is with me. That promise is part of the gift of Christmas: Emmanuel, God with us.

Lord, thank you that you never leave me, nor forsake me. Help me to trust that you are with me always. Help me to draw strength and courage from your presence in my life. Amen

---

1. *Why? Making Sense of God's Will* (Abingdon Press, 2011)
2. Psalm 23:4
3. For a more detailed discussion of this word from the prophets, see *The Journey: Walking the Road to Bethlehem*, the book that accompanies this book of reflections.

13. Joseph Did What the Lord Commanded
Matthew 1:24-25

When Joseph awoke from sleep, he did as the angel of the Lord commanded him; he took her as his wife, but had no marital relations with her until she had borne a son; and he named him Jesus.

JOSEPH WAS PERHAPS FIFTEEN OR SIXTEEN YEARS OLD when he was engaged to Mary.[1] We know from Scripture that at first he did not believe Mary's explanation of how she came to be pregnant. Though Joseph undoubtedly was hurt when Mary told him, he sought to spare her public embarrassment or, worse, death by stoning; and therefore he had determined to break off the engagement without explanation, taking the blame himself. But then he slept on it. And in his sleep Joseph dreamed of a messenger from God who assured him that Mary was telling the truth, that the child would save his people from their sins, and that Joseph was to marry her. Then comes this powerful line of Scripture: "When Joseph awoke from sleep, he did as the angel of the Lord commanded him."

This statement—like Mary's words, "Here am I, the servant of the Lord; let it be with me according to your word"[2]—is remarkable. Joseph chose to set aside his doubts about Mary's story. (Do you think he ever still had doubts? After all, the angel appeared to him in a dream. I would have needed more than a dream to erase all my doubts.) He decided to commit himself to raising a child destined to be a king. In obeying the angel in his dream, Joseph may have been sacrificing his own dreams for his future, his career, and his family. He would adopt the boy as his own. He would give up his father's carpentry shop in Bethlehem to relocate to Mary's hometown of Nazareth. These decisions would lead to Joseph's fleeing with Mary and the child to Egypt as refugees to save them from Herod. Surely, none of this was how Joseph had imagined his life.

Typically life does not unfold the way we dreamed it would. We move, marry, begin careers; but seldom do these things work out exactly as we had planned. John Lennon captured it well when he wrote, "Life is what happens to you while you're busy making other plans."[3]

It appears that Joseph did not live to see that thousands of people came to Jesus during his lifetime to learn of God's kingdom. He did not know the impact Jesus would have upon the world. But that impact was shaped by an earthly father who "did as the angel of the Lord commanded him" and gave up his own dreams to follow through with the marriage and raise a very special son.

My mom and dad conceived me when they were still in high school. Each had dreams of what they would do with their lives. Neither had anticipated that it would include getting married at ages seventeen and eighteen, bypassing college to raise a child, and working multiple jobs to make ends meet. My dad would work seventy and eighty hours a week. My mom, too, worked to support us. Even in 1964 they had choices that would have kept their dreams alive. The fact that I am alive today is because of their willingness to give up their dreams and to do what they felt God was asking them to do. How could I ever thank them for it?

Sometimes life's disappointments, the curveballs and detours, are a part of God's greater plan. Our task is to be willing, like Joseph, to "do as the . . . Lord commanded."

Lord, guide my life. When my dreams get in the way of your dreams for me, help me to understand. Grant me the courage, O God, to pursue your dreams for my life. Amen.

1. See the book that goes with these reflections for an alternative tradition in which Joseph was believed to be an elderly man when these events took place.
2. Luke 1:38
3. "Beautiful Boy (Darling Boy)," by John Lennon, © The David Geffen Company

14. Elizabeth Said to Her, "Blessed Are You . . ."

Luke 1:39-45

In those days Mary set out and went with haste to a Judean town in the hill country, where she entered the house of Zechariah and greeted Elizabeth. When Elizabeth heard Mary's greeting, the child leaped in her womb. And Elizabeth was filled with the Holy Spirit and exclaimed with a loud cry, "Blessed are you among women, and blessed is the fruit of your womb. And why has this happened to me, that the mother of my Lord comes to me? For as soon as I heard the sound of your greeting, the child in my womb leaped for joy. And blessed is she who believed that there would be a fulfillment of what was spoken to her by the Lord."

THERE ARE SOME THINGS YOU CAN'T REALLY APPRECIATE in the Scriptures until you've visited the Holy Land. I always read this passage from Luke and pictured young Mary leaving Nazareth and traveling for an hour or two until she arrived at Elizabeth's home. But as I was preparing this book, I traveled to the Holy Land and retraced Mary's steps from the Annunciation to the birth of Jesus. I was surprised to discover that Mary's journey to Elizabeth's home would have taken her eight to ten days. This was no small journey for a thirteen-year-old girl to make without her family.

I understand the Scriptures to be telling us that when Mary made the journey to Ein Karem, she had not yet told her family about her pregnancy. She "went with haste" because she was frightened and uncertain if there was anyone in the world who would believe her story. But she had just learned that her older cousin Elizabeth was pregnant despite being beyond childbearing years. Elizabeth was the one woman who might believe her. Then, after telling Elizabeth, she probably went next to

Joseph, who lived in Bethlehem, just a few miles away.

The traditional location for Elizabeth and Zechariah's home is Ein Karem. The town, mentioned several times in the Old Testament, is located on a hill a short distance from Jerusalem and just a few miles from Bethlehem. There are two churches on the hill, marking the traditional locations of Elizabeth's home and the place of John the Baptist's birth. The church higher up the hill is the Church of the Visitation, and it celebrates the story from our Scripture today.

As soon as Mary arrived in Ein Karem, Elizabeth immediately prophesied over her. Without being told, Elizabeth knew that Mary was pregnant and that the child would be the messianic king. Elizabeth thrice blessed Mary. Can you imagine what Elizabeth's words felt like to Mary? For nine days she had been traveling, carrying this secret with her and wondering if she would be put to death once it became known. For nine days she had imagined what it will be like to live with the shame of conceiving a child outside of wedlock. For nine days she had worried about how Joseph would respond. For nine days she had felt cursed by a burden too heavy for her to bear. And then, three times in as many sentences, Elizabeth had joyfully pronounced her blessed by God.

Elizabeth helped Mary see her situation through the eyes of faith. She helped Mary recognize blessing where others would have only seen a burden. She infused Mary with hope.

Several years ago I had the opportunity to tour the American Stroke Foundation[1] and meet stroke survivors, volunteers, and staff. I learned that most of the people who die after experiencing a severe stroke don't die from the stroke itself; they die because they lose hope, become depressed, and give up. By contrast, it was amazing to see the hope of the people at the Foundation. The place was filled with Elizabeths—staff, volunteers, and fellow patients—giving stroke survivors hope and the willpower to keep pressing on. This was no Pollyanna attitude that minimizes adversity, but a deliberate choice to see the possible, and the blessing, in the midst of adversity.

This type of support and encouragement is precisely what Elizabeth gave Mary in calling her blessed. And it is what we have the opportunity to do when, with compassion and understanding, we help others find blessings and hope in the face of the burdens they bear.

Lord, help me to embody good news and to bless those who are struggling. Use me to offer hope and encouragement to those who are weary and heavy laden. Amen.

---

1. http://www.americanstroke.org/

15. How Mary Found Her Joy
Luke 1:46-47

And Mary said, "My soul magnifies the Lord, and my spirit rejoices in God my Savior."

FOR NINE OR TEN DAYS MARY had carried in her heart the most astounding secret: She was pregnant, and the child was to be the long-awaited messianic king, Israel's deliverer. Yet she had been afraid to share the news, for if the wrong person heard, Herod could have had her killed; or, if her loved ones didn't believe her, the religious leaders might have condemned her and had her put to death. Perhaps she herself was afraid to trust that it was true.

But when Elizabeth prophesied over Mary and announced that she was blessed, Mary finally was able to trust that God really was at work. She believed that, despite the inherent danger in carrying the Messiah, despite the reality that her hopes and dreams had been turned upside down, and despite the fact that she didn't fully understand, God would work through her and her child. In her acceptance of this amazing truth, Mary finally shouted out her song of joy. Can you hear the tone of her song in its opening words? "My soul magnifies the Lord! My spirit rejoices in God my Savior!"

Joy, unlike happiness, can come to us independent of our circumstances. It comes not from changing our circumstances but from viewing them through the eyes of faith. The apostles, after being beaten by the Council, rejoiced because they were counted worthy to suffer for the name of Jesus. Paul penned his well-known "epistle of joy"—the Letter to the Philippians—even as he sat in a

Roman prison awaiting news as to whether he would be executed for his faith. In the letter he wrote, "Rejoice in the Lord always!" Paul wrote to the Christians at Thessalonica, who themselves had been persecuted for their faith, "Rejoice always," and then told them how this was possible when he continued, "Pray without ceasing" and "give thanks in all circumstances."[1]

Last year I was in Malawi, Africa, visiting rural villages to explore partnerships with local congregations to build wells, schools, and churches. In one of the villages, the people, who earn about fifty-five cents per person per day, took us to the stream of green, brackish water that they used for drinking, cooking, and cleaning. They asked us to consider helping them build a well so their children might not get sick from the water anymore.

After we had toured their village, they invited us to their church. We stepped inside the mud-brick building. It was just a large room with open holes where windows might go, and daylight shining through gaps in the thatched roof. And then they began to worship. They sang songs of utter joy, despite their circumstances. They sang songs of joy because they trusted God, and they believed that God had brought us to Malawi to help them have safe drinking water (something we ourselves believed). Would that Christians in the United States sang with such exuberance and joy!

Mary, despite dangers, fears, risks, and upended dreams, "magnified the Lord and rejoiced in God." She did this with the help of Elizabeth and with her own willingness to trust that God was working in and through her to accomplish his purposes.

Joy is a choice we make when we look at our present circumstances through the eyes of faith, trusting that God is at work and that he will never leave us nor abandon us. And it is often found with the help of another who reassures us that God is with us.

Lord, I thank you, even now, for your blessings in my life. Help me to see past my circumstances, to what you will do with and through them. Help me to trust you. Use my adversity for your glory. Amen.

---

1. Philippians 4:4; 1 Thessalonians 5:16-17

16. A Most Unnerving Song
Luke 1:48-53

He has looked with favor on the lowliness of his servant.
Surely, from now on all generations will call me blessed;
for the Mighty One has done great things for me,
and holy is his name.
His mercy is for those who fear him
from generation to generation.
He has shown strength with his arm;
he has scattered the proud in the thoughts of their hearts.
He has brought down the powerful from their thrones,
and lifted up the lowly;
he has filled the hungry with good things,
and sent the rich away empty.

AFTER HEARING ELIZABETH'S BLESSING, Mary broke out into a song of joy. She cried out, "My soul magnifies the Lord!" But many stop at the opening line and fail to realize how subversive, even revolutionary, Mary's song really was. Remember, Mary was a thirteen-year-old peasant girl from a town of people who were on the lower rungs of the socioeconomic ladder. It was Herod and his supporters, along with the Romans and those of the upper class who were allied with them, who ruled the land. Yet God chose Mary to give birth to the messianic king.

I think back to the wedding of Prince William and Princess Kate in the spring of 2011. Now, there was a princess of a respected family. But Mary? She was from Nazareth. She was a nobody. But she understood that this was God's way. He chose as the mother of his Son a lowly peasant girl from a working-class family. Can you feel her utter amazement? her joy?

Mary's psalm began to take on a revolutionary note when she sang, "He has scattered the proud in the thoughts of their hearts. He has brought down the powerful from their thrones, and lifted up the lowly." As I read these words I think, "Yes, that is how God works. 'He humbles the proud but gives grace to the humble.'" The proud had it coming. I immediately think of the tyrants in the Middle East who were overthrown in what was dubbed the Facebook Revolution in the spring of 2011.

The next two lines of Mary's song always leave me feeling disturbed: "He has filled the hungry with good things, and sent the rich away empty." It is one thing to speak of God humbling the proud, but sending the rich away empty? This begins to feel uncomfortable. Today, many would read this line to be suggesting a redistribution of wealth and might accuse Mary of the "s-word": *socialism*.

Mary's words should make us uncomfortable. They point to a concern God has for the poor, and a sense that the rich have received theirs already. Since the income of the average American puts us in the top five percent in per-capita income in the world, most of us are "rich." Here's how I read these words in Mary's song. They are a reminder of something Jesus said later: "To whom much has been given, much will be required."[1] Jesus' words are a reminder of the call upon Abraham, who was "blessed to be a blessing."

To the degree that we earn our money unjustly, or hoard it without being willing to share, we do have reason to be anxious about the day when we give an account of our lives. But we have a choice. We can choose to "do justice, and to love kindness, and to walk humbly with [our] God."[2] We have the obligation and the calling to be used by God to "fill the hungry with good things." When we do these things, we need not fear being sent away empty.

When I think of Mary's song, I'm reminded of a young woman named Gracie. At the age of eleven she heard me preach about the people in southern Africa and our church's plans to build fish ponds in rural African villages so the hungry could be fed. Her heart was touched. Gracie had been taking voice lessons and, at age eleven, was already writing songs. She asked her parents if she could record a CD and sell it to her friends and family to raise money for fish ponds. God blessed her efforts, and Gracie had the opportunity to sing for various churches and events. As of the writing of this book, Gracie is thirteen, about the age Mary likely was when she went to Elizabeth, and so far Gracie has raised twenty thousand dollars to build two fish ponds in Africa and to support an orphanage with twelve boys in Haiti.[3]

Gracie's songs, and what she's done with the proceeds of her CD sales, are a picture of what Mary's song looks like, lived out. How might God be calling you to use your gifts to send the hungry away filled?

Lord, help me to see how I might use the gifts you've given me to "do justice, and to love kindness, and to walk humbly" with you. Help me, like Gracie, to send the hungry away filled. Amen.

---

1. Luke 12:48
2. Micah 6:8
3. You can find out more about Gracie and purchase her music by visiting her Web site at www.gracieschram.com.

17. Who Is Your Mary?
Who Is Your Elizabeth?
Luke 1:56

And Mary remained with her about three months and then returned to her home.

ON THE APPROACH TO THE CHURCH of the Visitation in Ein Karem, Israel, the hillsides are covered with olive trees. The church itself is built atop an ancient cistern where it is claimed Mary drew water for Elizabeth. The church celebrates the role these two women played in each other's lives. Frescoes, mosaics, paintings, and sculptures abound showing Mary and Elizabeth together. Elizabeth was probably in her late fifties or early sixties when Mary came to visit and was in her sixth month of pregnancy. (She was beyond natural childbearing years, and it is implied in

Luke that she only became pregnant by the miraculous intervention of God.) Mary was likely thirteen and was just beginning her first month of pregnancy.

Mary stayed with Elizabeth for the final three months of Elizabeth's pregnancy. One can imagine Mary helping with things around the home, doing all the things Elizabeth may typically have done. Elizabeth undoubtedly found Mary a help both physically and emotionally. The two women shared in common unusual pregnancies that could only be explained as the act of God.

Mary found great joy and comfort in being with her older cousin Elizabeth. Here was a motherly (or grandmotherly) figure who loved Mary, encouraged and mentored her, and helped her through those first three months of pregnancy. Each needed the other. Each was blessed by the other.

The Church of the Visitation is a celebration of women's friendships, their sisterhood, and the close bonds that are possible when women care for one another. Those themes can be seen in the art adorning the building, such as a bronze sculpture of the two women, one barely showing her pregnancy and the other well along, that sits in the courtyard outside the church. I found it interesting to stand watching the pilgrims and tourists coming to visit. The vast majority were women. I observed a bus full of African women as they arrived, dressed colorfully and filled with laughter. They would look at the statue and then take each other's hands, or embrace, and you could see the love and friendship they shared. I was asked to come and take their pictures as they stood—smiling, laughing, sharing together—next to the statue of Mary and Elizabeth.

It struck me as I stood there that Elizabeth and Mary's story points to the importance of having friendships that span generations. The older mentor the younger, and the younger encourage and bring vitality to the older. The older bring wisdom, the younger energy, dreams, and fresh perspectives.

This is important not just to women, but to men as well. I have had several older mentors through the years, men who encouraged me, invested in me, believed in me, and counseled me. I have had the privilege of seeking to encourage, befriend, and bless them as well. As I moved into my forties, I found myself being approached by younger pastors who were looking for mentors, and I became conscious of the fact that at some point our task is to invest in and encourage a new generation.

Among the women I know who have been amazing Elizabeths is a woman named Marty Mather. Marty is in her early eighties but shows no signs of slowing down. She teaches multiple Bible studies and corresponds with dozens or even hundreds of people. She is constantly pouring wisdom and encouragement into the lives of others.

Among Marty's gifts is baking the most delicious homemade bread you could ever eat. She invites groups of younger women to join her for bread-baking classes. After handing out her recipe and teaching her pupils how to prepare the dough, she has them leave it to rise, and during that time she gathers them in a circle and invites them to share their stories. Then she shares her own story, including the story of her deep Methodist faith.

Marty's boundless energy comes from these younger women (and men) whom she mentors and encourages. She is blessed by these friendships. And those who sit under her tutelage find that they have an amazing treasure in her love, encouragement, and wisdom.

We all need an Elizabeth we can turn to for advice, wisdom, and encouragement. And we're all called to be an Elizabeth for someone else—to invest in that person and pass on what we've learned. Do you have an Elizabeth? And who is the Mary you are mentoring?

Lord, thank you for those older than I am who have invested in my life. Help me to encourage and bless those who are my seniors. But help me too, Lord, to bless and encourage those who are younger than I. Amen.

18. The Unplanned Wedding That Scripture Doesn't Mention Luke 2:3-4

All went to their own towns to be registered. Joseph also went from the town of Nazareth in Galilee.

IN MATTHEW, WE LAST SAW JOSEPH in Bethlehem. In Luke, Mary was in Ein Karem. Matthew tells us that when Joseph awoke from the dream in which he was instructed to wed Mary, "he did what the angel of the Lord commanded him" and took Mary home as his wife. The text presupposes, I believe, that this took place in Bethlehem. Yet Luke tells us they ended up in Nazareth; for, as Mary's pregnancy drew to a close, a census required them to travel to Bethlehem. So, were they married in

Bethlehem or Nazareth? In the companion book to these reflections, I suggest that after spending three months at Ein Karem with Elizabeth, Mary returned to Nazareth, Joseph joined her, and they were married in Nazareth in a "hurry up" wedding.

I officiated at the wedding of our oldest daughter, Danielle, a couple of years ago. It was an exciting and emotional time. She invited us to join her in picking out flowers, planning the menu for the reception, and selecting her dress. Invitations, reservations, and a thousand other details went into the planning of the wedding, most of which were carried out by my wife and daughter. I had the joy of writing the check! The night of the rehearsal I was a wreck. I kept thinking back to the times when Danielle was little and I would dance with her in my arms; or the time she told me I was her hero; or the way she said she would love me "from here to Jupiter and back again." And now I was giving her away. I still get emotional thinking about it.

We can be sure that Mary and Joseph's wedding did not take place the way anyone had planned. The original plans would have been canceled and a hasty wedding and reception put together. Guests would have understood why the wedding date was moved up. They would have believed that Joseph had taken advantage of Mary, or that Mary and Joseph had been unable to control their passions. This would have been the gossip of the town and perhaps a source of embarrassment to Mary's parents.

Yet Mary and Joseph had done nothing wrong. In fact, they were models of faithfulness and devotion to God. They were obedient, and their obedience came at great personal cost. Yet others could not understand this.

Have you ever done something that you felt God was calling you to do but that caused others to question your motives, integrity, or actions? Or perhaps you've had people gossip about you. If so, you are in good company. This surely would have been a part of Mary and Joseph's story.

The truth is, it is human nature to pass judgment on others, to share "juicy" gossip, and to assume the worst about others. Perhaps this story, and our own experiences, might lead us to recall the words of Jesus when he taught his followers to "take the log out of your own eye" before taking the splinter out of your neighbor's eye. He taught them to "do not judge, so that you may not be judged." And he told them, "Blessed are you when people insult you and persecute you and utter all kinds of evil against you falsely on my account."[1] Is it possible these words of Jesus were shaped in part by the way people whispered about his mother when he was just a child?

Lord, help me not to judge others nor to participate in gossip. And help me to forgive when others have questioned my motives, my actions, or my heart. Amen.

---

1. See Matthew 7:1-5; 5:11.

19. The Journeys We Don't Want to Take

Luke 2:1-5

In those days a decree went out from Emperor Augustus that all the world should be registered. This was the first registration and was taken while Quirinius was governor of Syria. All went to their own towns to be registered. Joseph also went from the town of Nazareth in Galilee to Judea, to the city of David called Bethlehem, because he was descended from the house and family of David. He went to be registered with Mary, to whom he was engaged and who was expecting a child.

WE COME TO THE JOURNEY Mary and Joseph made from Nazareth to Bethlehem, when Mary was "great with child." This certainly was not a journey that Mary and

Joseph wanted to take. They undoubtedly had planned to have the baby in Nazareth. The midwife would have been chosen and the birthing room prepared. But when the Roman emperor commanded that a census be taken, he wasn't concerned about a Jewish family preparing to give birth. He was interested in assessing taxes.

In the fall of 2010, while in the Holy Land, I retraced the journey of Mary and Joseph by following the most direct route from Nazareth to Bethlehem. Along the way I was struck by how difficult the journey must have been for Mary, and how disappointing. I was also reminded that this was only the first of several journeys she did not want to take with Jesus. She would also flee as a refugee to Egypt when Herod sought to kill the child. And years later she would make the same journey from Nazareth with Jesus, as he went to Jerusalem where he would be nailed to a cross.

Like Mary, all of us find ourselves forced to take journeys we do not wish to make. These journeys are not prescribed by God but by life's circumstances or the will of others. In the midst of them we may be disappointed; wonder if we've been abandoned by God; or simply feel confused as to why we've had to travel such roads. Perhaps Mary felt some of these same emotions on the journey to Bethlehem.

But here's what we find in Scripture and what is echoed in our own lives: God does not abandon us while we're on these journeys. Somehow, in ways we never anticipated, he even works through them. We look back years later and can see how God took adversity, disappointment, and pain and used these very things to accomplish his purposes.

Ann was five months pregnant when she sensed that something was not right. After an amniocentesis, doctors diagnosed her unborn baby with a genetic condition called "Chromosome 22 Ring." At the time, very few other cases were known. The doctors told Ann and her husband, Jerry, that their child would likely be stillborn. When she asked about delivering the child early so doctors might have a chance to perform a surgery that might save his life, the doctors came back and said, "Ann, this will not be a life worth saving." Ann and Jerry would remember those words many times over the years.

Matthew was born in January 1984. Ann and Jerry chose the name *Matthew* because it means "gift from the Lord." Matthew was born with several serious birth defects, but he lived. This was not a journey Ann and Jerry had anticipated or would have desired to make, but it was the journey life had dealt them, and they were grateful for their son.

I first met Matthew when he was eight. His mom and dad visited our church, and out of that visit our church started a ministry for Matthew and children like him, a special-needs ministry that we named after him: Matthew's Ministry. Later, when Matthew needed surgery, knowing he would need blood, his surgery prompted us to start an annual blood drive.

Matthew died at the age of twenty-one. His life shaped Ann and Jerry into two of the most remarkable people I know. And Matthew changed thousands of other lives. Today, over 140 special-needs children and adults are a part of our Matthew's Ministry. Annually in our blood drives we collect over fifteen hundred pints of blood for people in the Kansas City area. Our church and community were changed as a result of this child whose life "wasn't worth saving."

God's greatest work often arises out of the journeys we don't want to take. God has a way of wringing good from disappointment, suffering, and pain. This is what Ann and Jerry found. It is what Joseph and Mary came to see again and again. Look back over your life. Can you see how God brought good from adversity? If you are on such a journey right now, trust God to walk with you and to bring good from it.

Lord, thank you for the way you bring good from suffering. Please help me to remember that you promised never to leave me nor forsake me. Bring good from the adversity in my life, and grant me your peace when I take those journeys I don't want to take. Amen.

20. No Room in the Guest Room Luke 2:6-7

While they were there, the time came for her to deliver her child. And she gave birth to her firstborn son and wrapped him in bands of cloth, and laid him in a manger, because there was no place for them in the inn.

AFTER TEN DAYS OF TRAVEL, Joseph and Mary finally arrived in Bethlehem. But upon arriving, the young couple found the local inn overcrowded, so Mary was forced to give birth in a barn. Right? Maybe, but maybe not.

The word translated in most English versions as "inn" is the Greek word *kataluma*. This word can also be, and perhaps should be, translated as "guest room." The word appears in two other places in the New Testament, in Mark and Luke, when Jesus tells his disciples on Thursday of Holy Week to find the owner of a particular house and ask, "Where is the guest room (*kataluma*) where I may eat the Passover with my disciples?" The word referred to an extra room in a house.

I've suggested that Joseph was from Bethlehem. Why would he need an inn if his family lived there? He would not. Many scholars also suggest it is unlikely that there was an inn in Bethlehem. A better translation of Luke 2:7 might be that she laid him in a manger because "there was no place for them in the guest room."

Joseph's entire family would have been required to return to Bethlehem for the census. Most would have arrived before Mary and Joseph, so the guest room likely would already have had two or three families staying in it. But there also would have been a stable or barn in the house—tradition says it was a cave like the one at

Mary's home in Nazareth. It makes sense to think that Mary and Joseph would have been afforded greater privacy, and would have avoided making the rest of the house ceremonially unclean, by staying in that stable or barn. Therefore Mary laid her son in a manger, because "there was no place for them in the guest room."

Luke doesn't explain all this to us. That is not his point. What he wants us to notice is that Mary gave birth in a makeshift shelter and Jesus' first bed was a feeding trough. The King of kings was born to a young couple whose income placed them on the lowest rung of society, and he was born homeless.

Christianity speaks of Jesus' birth as the "Incarnation"; that is, in Jesus, God came and lived among us. Jesus' birth, life, teachings, death, and resurrection all show us God's heart and character. In Jesus' birthplace, we see that the God of the universe identifies with the lowly. This leads me to love him even more. This is the glory of God that we see in Jesus Christ—humility, compassion, mercy, tenderness, and lowliness.

Today, as many as 3.5 million Americans are homeless at some point during the year. Of these, thirty-nine percent are under the age of eighteen.[1] A surprising number of homeless women are pregnant. Part of God's message in Christmas is intended for those who are homeless or nearly so. In Christmas, God says to them, "When I came to walk on earth, I was born in a stable, to two teenage parents who had nowhere else to stay."

As you prepare for Christmas you've likely been shopping, trying to buy gifts for people who already have all they need. What if this year you gave gifts in honor of your friends and family to help people who really are in need? My friend, Pastor Mike Slaughter, likes to remind his congregation, "Christmas is not your birthday!" He challenges everyone in his congregation to give to the poor each Christmas an amount equal to what they will spend on their family. My wife, LaVon, and I began doing this several years ago. Our decision acts as a governor on what we spend for our family, keeps us focused on what Christmas is really about, and fills us with the joy of knowing we are helping others.

I challenge you to consider doing this in your own life or with your family. Your local church likely has suggestions for you of projects to serve those in need this Christmas.

Lord, I am humbled that you came to us as a child born in a stable and laid to sleep in a manger. Help me to see those in need as you see them, and this Christmas to serve as your hands and voice to bless them in your name. Amen.

1. National Coalition for the Homeless, July 2009, http://www.nationalhome less.org/factsheets/How_Many.html Accessed June 2, 2011.

21. Night-Shift Shepherds

Luke 2:8

In that region there were shepherds living in the fields, keeping watch over their flock by night.

GARRISON KEILLOR WRITES THE FOLLOWING description of shepherds in his foreword to Ron Parker's *The Sheep Book: A Handbook for the Modern Shepherd*: "They are gentle and attentive people and good company . . . shepherding is an ancient scientific culture and teaches people more than they intended to learn and brings out qualities in them they might not attain directly through moral ambition."[1]

In Jesus' time, shepherds were absolutely essential suppliers of wool, milk, meat, and sacrifices; but they were not held in high esteem among the townsfolk. Some people considered them backward and simple, and they were often seen as uneducated, unsophisticated, and unclean. In speaking with Palestinians in Bethlehem during my recent trip, I was surprised to learn that this is still how shepherds are seen among many people to this day. Perhaps this is the very reason that God had an affinity for shepherds. God, like Garth Brooks, seems to enjoy "friends in low places."

What else do we learn about the shepherds in our story? We know these men were the night-shift shepherds. These were the lowest of the shepherds.

During my trip, I met with a shepherd named Ibrahim and his family, who make their living by keeping a dozen or so sheep in and around Bethlehem. Their humble state was evident as we talked.[2] I asked Ibrahim why God chose to invite the shepherds to be the first to see and celebrate the birth of Jesus. He responded instantly, "Because Jesus was humble, and shepherds are humble."

It may be that some of you reading this are thinking, "This author is like a broken record—in nearly every reflection he mentions God's choice of the humble in the Christmas story." But I don't believe this is my theme; it seems to be God's theme. The theme plays out over and over again in the story—from the choice of Mary of Nazareth, to the choice of a simple *lekton* in Bethlehem, to the song that Mary sang about the way God fills the hungry with good things, to the birth in a stable, to the choice of night-shift shepherds as the first people invited to celebrate the birth of Jesus.

James captures this idea when, quoting Proverbs 3:34, he writes, "God opposes the proud, but gives grace to the humble" (James 4:6). The response that this idea is meant to evoke is captured in James 4:10: "Humble yourselves before the Lord, and he will exalt you." The apostle Paul offers similar words of admonition in Philippians 2:3: "Do nothing from selfish ambition or conceit, but in humility regard others as better than yourselves."

Among the people I know who exemplify this spirit is a physician in Kansas City named Gary Morsch. Gary is one of the founders of Heart to Heart, an organization that delivers medical supplies and more to impoverished countries and disaster areas. One of Gary's lessons in humility came when he went to visit Mother Teresa's mission in Calcutta, India. He and his team arrived to deliver medicine and to care for patients at the Home for the Dying and Destitute. Gary, stethoscope around his neck, introduced himself to Sister Priscilla as a physician from the United States who was ready to help the sisters. She said, "Follow me, please," and proceeded to escort him through the wards of dying people to the kitchen, where there was a large pile of putrefying garbage. She said to him, "We need you to take this garbage to the dump. The dump is several blocks down the street."

In an instant, doctor was demoted to garbage man. As Gary made trip after trip to the dump, he began to feel sorry for himself, resenting the fact that he had come all the way to Calcutta, delivered millions of dollars in medicine, was a physician with a stethoscope in his back pocket to prove it, and yet was hauling garbage. After having done this for several hours, he noticed a small sign with Mother Teresa's famous words: "We can do no great things, only small things with great love." It was then that he understood why he had been assigned garbage duty. It was God's way of teaching him humility, servanthood, and love.[3]

If God chose night-shift shepherds to be the first to celebrate the birth of Christ, what might that tell you about the attitude of heart that God is looking for from you and me?

Lord, thank you that you humble the proud and give grace to the humble. Help me to humble myself before you and to do nothing from selfish ambition or conceit, but in humility to consider others better than myself. Amen.

---

1. From Garrison Keillor's forward to Ron Parker's, *The Sheep Book: A Handbook for the Modern Shepherd* (Scribners, 1983), p. ix
2. A small portion of my interview with Ibrahim is featured in session 5 of the videos that are available to accompany these reflections.
3. Gary is a deeply committed Christian whom I consider a friend. He has written an excellent book entitled *The Power of Serving Others* (Berrett-Koehler Publishing, 2006). You can find the above story in more detail on pages 18-20.

22. A Message to the Shepherds

Luke 2:8-11

In that region there were shepherds living in the fields, keeping watch over their flock by night. Then an angel of the Lord stood before them, and the glory of the Lord shone around them, and they were terrified. But the angel said to them, "Do not be afraid; for see—I am bringing you good news of great joy for all the people: to you is born this day in the city of David a Savior, who is the Messiah, the Lord."

WHILE THE SHEPHERDS WERE WATCHING over their flocks, a messenger from God appeared to them. The sight of a complete stranger in the middle of the night on a hillside in Bethlehem would have been enough to startle these shepherds; but Luke also tells us "the glory of the Lord shone around them." What is the glory of the Lord? Sometimes in Scripture the expression is synonymous with God's presence, sometimes his character, sometimes his attributes. There are times, however, when God's glory refers to something visible, and this seems to be the case here. What did it look like? Luke doesn't tell us, but Exodus 24:17 notes that "the appearance of the glory of the LORD was like a devouring fire." Ezekiel, when he saw the glory of the Lord, described "something that looked like fire," followed by a rainbow (1:26-28). Whatever the shepherds saw, their response was to be "sore afraid."

But the angel told them not to be afraid, for he was bringing them "good news of great joy for all the people." I love that phrase. Christmas is good news of great joy for all the people. What is this good news? It is the fact that a Savior has come to rule the earth.

The Greek word for savior, *soter*, means one who offers help and deliverance for those in trouble. Warriors, rulers, even some of the Greco-Roman gods were considered saviors. In Luke's story, the night-shift shepherds were being invited to see the newborn Savior, King, and Lord.

Christmas celebrates the birth of the one who came to save the human race from sin. Remember, sin is the propensity to do, and the actually doing of, those things that are counter to God's will in our individual lives and collectively as a race. Jesus came to save us from judgment, from separation from God, from guilt and shame. But he also came to show us a different way to live—to show us what it means to be human and what God's will is for our lives. He came to invite us to follow him, to be changed by him, and thus to be saved by him.

A group of former prostitutes and drug addicts arrive at our church by van each week for worship. They come from one of our urban ministry partners called the Healing House. I love this ministry, as well as the women and men who are a part of it. Bobbi Jo is the founder. A former prostitute and addict, she describes her life before she came to faith in Christ: She had been on the streets for years, during which time she had been raped sixteen times and had twenty-four broken bones. Ultimately she ended up in detox, and about that time Bobbi Jo finally asked God to help her, deliver her, and save her. And God did. She found hope and strength, and her heart and life began to change. When her mother died, Bobbi Jo was left with a small inheritance that she used to start the Healing House.

Today, seventy people live in the three buildings that are part of this ministry. These women and men have come to a place where they, too, are asking God to save them. They are seeing him change their lives. In turn, they seek to live as followers of Jesus, and the world is changed by this. Each of their lives is like a stone cast into a pond: the ripples expand in every direction.

Every time I see this group in worship, I feel as if they are living, breathing testimony to the good news of great joy to all the people, that at the first Christmas a child was born to be the Savior, the Messiah, the Lord.

Christ still saves us. He forgives, heals, and changes us. He is still Lord, calling us to follow him each day of our lives. Take a moment today to invite him to continue saving you from the ways in which you stray from God's path, and pledge to follow him as your Lord.

Jesus, save me. Save me from the guilt I sometimes feel for my past sins and mistakes. Forgive me. And Jesus, save me from my tendency to turn from God's path today and every day. I wish to follow you as my Lord. Lead me on your path. Amen.

23. The Angelic Chorus
Luke 2:12-14

"This will be a sign for you: you will find a child wrapped in bands of cloth and lying in a manger." And suddenly there was with the angel a multitude of the heavenly host, praising God and saying, "Glory to God in the highest heaven, and on earth peace among those whom he favors!"

THE SHEPHERDS WERE ON THE HILLSIDES not far from Bethlehem. When you visit Bethlehem, one of the places you may be taken is the "shepherd's fields"—two hillsides separated by a valley. The ruins of ancient churches dot one hill, as well as two chapels and an interesting cave that gives you a glimpse of what a cave dwelling may have looked like at the time of Jesus. You'll also likely see, down in the valley, a shepherd or two grazing some sheep.

After the messenger of the Lord had explained that the Savior had been born, he encouraged the shepherds to leave behind their sheep and go to Bethlehem to see the Christ Child. They were to look for a newborn child, wrapped in bands of cloth and lying in a feeding trough for animals (a manger). What a sign! They would find the Savior of the world not by a star—that was the sign for the magi—but by finding a child laid to sleep in a makeshift crib!

And then, suddenly, as if the heavens could no longer keep quiet, a host of strangers appeared, singing and praising God. I wonder if you've seen the video of the "flash mob" singing the Hallelujah Chorus in a mall food court. An unsuspecting crowd of people are eating their lunch in the food court when one woman begins to sing, "Hallelujah! Hallelujah! Hal-le-lu-jah!" Then another joins her, and another, and another, until several dozen people are singing together in perfect harmony as a stunned crowd watches. This is how I picture the angelic chorus appearing and breaking into song that first Christmas night.

In the shepherds' fields, the heavenly chorus sang, "Glory to God in the highest heaven, and on earth peace among those whom he favors." The order of these two ideas may be important. First comes praise, and then comes peace. Glory to God. Peace on earth. I find in my own life, as I praise God, I begin to experience God's peace. When I'm frightened or anxious or feeling down, I sing hymns and choruses. Sometimes, when I remember the tune but not the words to a hymn, I make up my own words. But the act of singing God's praise gives me God's peace. I've also found that singing God's praise to others often gives them peace.

Years ago, while I was serving as the youth director of a church in Texas, I took the youth to do repairs at the homes of two elderly women living in a blighted south Dallas neighborhood. Some of the other homes in their neighborhood were boarded up. Some had been torn down. Some were drug houses. These women had lived in this neighborhood for decades, but the world seemed to have forgotten them.

The women were excited when we arrived. As we scraped and caulked and painted their homes, they prepared cookies and lemonade and told us stories of their lives. These women knew they were teaching the youth that day. When we left their homes they were so grateful, and our youth were filled with joy.

The following Christmas, we decided to take the kids back one night to carol for these two women. Our youth took up an offering among themselves to give the women, and from their own money they collected two hundred dollars for each woman. They all signed Christmas cards for the women and tucked the money inside.

I'll never forget what happened at one of these homes. We emptied the bus, and forty-five youth stood around the doorstep of Miss Violet's home. We began to sing, and as we did it seemed the whole neighborhood came outside to see what was happening. It had been a long time since any of them had seen a caroler on that street. Miss Violet turned on the front light and slowly opened the door as we sang. Then one of the youth stepped forward and presented her with gifts and the card. The young woman said, "Miss Violet, we came to remind you that God loves you. These gifts are a sign of his love and ours, too. Merry Christmas!"

Miss Violet stood there, dumbfounded. Her hands shaking, she opened the card and read it, then looked at the money that fell into her hands. Tears began to roll down her cheeks, and she said in almost a whisper, "Ever since my husband died, I thought God had forgotten me. Tonight, you reminded me that he still remembers I'm here." It was one of the most moving experiences in my ministry at that church.

I wonder if this is what the night-shift shepherds felt that night, as the heavenly host sang carols to them.

Lord, help me to be one of your angels, reminding others of the "good news of great joy" that is Christmas. Help me, with my words and deeds, to be a visible sign that you love those around me. Amen.

24. The Shepherds' Response
Luke 2:15-20

When the angels had left them and gone into heaven, the shepherds said to one another, "Let us go now to Bethlehem and see this thing that has taken place, which the Lord has made known to us." So they went with haste and found Mary and Joseph, and the child lying in the manger. When they saw this, they made known what had been told them about this child; and all who heard it were amazed at what the shepherds told them. But Mary treasured all these words and pondered them in her heart. The shepherds returned, glorifying and praising God for all they had heard and seen, as it had been told them.

THE SHEPHERDS HAD HEARD FROM heavenly messengers that a new king had been born in Bethlehem. They would find him in a parking garage (that's what a stable was), lying in a bed of straw where the animals ate.

How would the shepherds respond? Would they stay in their fields; or would they leave their flocks, risk losing their jobs, and hike over the hillsides to Bethlehem in search of the newborn King? Scripture tells us what they did: The shepherds "went with haste" to see the one whose birth would be a source of "good news of great joy for all the people."

When the shepherds arrived, they saw with their own eyes "Mary and Joseph, and the child lying in the manger," and they became God's messengers—God's angels—telling others about the child. This is important. It demonstrates a rhythm in the Christian life: Others tell us about Jesus, we see with our own eyes and believe, and we tell others what we've seen. Then we return to our daily lives with joy, changed forever.

It is Christmas time, and there are many people who typically don't go to church but are searching nonetheless for the "good news of great joy for all the people." They've been searching at the mall, at their Christmas parties, even sitting in front of a decorated Christmas tree, but they still haven't found Christmas. And they won't find it, unless someone plays the part of the angel and invites them to come and see the child "wrapped in bands of cloth and lying in a manger."

Ann's husband invited her to attend our candlelight Christmas Eve services one year. She wrote, "If my husband hadn't invited me to Church of the Resurrection, I would still be searching for a way to fill the hole in my heart that God now fills." That was many years ago; today, Ann has gone on to become a leader in our congregation.

Each year, we give away our entire Christmas Eve offering to two projects benefiting children in poverty. Half of the funds last year went to projects in Malawi,

Africa, and the other half to renovate and support inner-city schools. Ann has become one of the leaders in our work with the inner-city schools, which includes tutoring, installing playgrounds, repainting buildings, and supporting teachers.

After we had completed a playground at one of the inner-city schools, a man at the school asked Ann, "Why would you do this for us?" She told him, "It's our way of showing God's love for you." Both began to cry as they stood on the playground that day.

Ann's angel was her husband, who invited her to "come and see." She came on Christmas Eve and heard the story of the child, born in a barn, who slept in a feeding trough. She discovered the "good news of great joy for all the people." When Ann returned home, "singing and praising God," she went on to became a messenger who has shared God's love with hundreds of others.

The world was changed because of that one invitation.

Who is God calling you to be a messenger for this Christmas?

Lord, please use me to invite _____ to Christmas Eve services this year. Make me one of your messengers. Then help _____ to hear the "good news of great joy" that you have come to us in Jesus Christ. Amen.

25. The Meaning of the Manger

Luke 2:12 and John 6:35

"This will be a sign for you: you will find a child wrapped in bands of cloth and lying in a manger."

"I am the bread of life. Whoever comes to me will never be hungry."

AFTER JESUS WAS BORN, he was wrapped in strips of cloth and placed in a manger. A manger is a feeding trough from which donkeys, horses, and other animals eat. While we usually picture the manger as constructed of wood, the only examples we have left in the Holy Land from ancient times are actually large stones that have been carved out on top to hold straw.

Luke mentions the manger three times in just a few verses as he tells the story of Jesus' birth. This is unusual and should lead us to ask why. Why does Luke feel it important to tell us about Jesus' first bed? And why does he mention it three times?

One reason is obvious: the manger points to Jesus' humble birth. It embodies a profoundly moving truth: that on his first night on this earth, the King of Glory, the Son of God, slept in a trough where the animals fed. What a picture of God's desire to identify with the humble and the poor.

But I think Luke had something more in mind, something I had not seen in twenty-five years of preaching the Christmas story. I believe Luke mentions the sign of the manger three times to communicate the powerful image of Jesus' first bed being the place where God's creatures come to eat.

Jesus was born in Bethlehem, a town that means "House of Bread." John would later describe Jesus multiplying the loaves of bread and saying, "I am the bread of life. Whoever comes to me will never be hungry" (John 6:35). Jesus was, of course, speaking of a spiritual sustenance the world would receive from him. Matthew, Mark, and Luke record Jesus taking bread at the Last Supper and saying, "This is my body, which is given for you." (See Luke 22:19.)

The manger—the feeding trough—was a sign of what Jesus came to do. He came to offer himself as bread for our souls. He came to satisfy a hunger that could not be satisfied any other way.

When Jesus was tested in the wilderness at the beginning of his ministry, the devil tempted him to turn stones into bread. But Jesus responded by quoting Deuteronomy 8:3, "One does not live by bread alone" (Luke 4:4). Yet one of our greatest struggles is that we forget this. We come to believe that if we have enough bread—enough money, enough stuff—we will be satisfied. But here's something I am absolutely certain of: there is nothing you or your family members will open on Christmas morning that will ultimately satisfy the deepest longings of your heart.

I have watched people in the congregation I serve who forgot this. They found that the "cares of this world and the desire for wealth" choked out the gospel. They lived their lives for more and bigger and better; but the more they had, the less they were satisfied, like someone with a disease that leaves them always hungry, and though they eat and eat and eat, they are never filled.

Our hearts hunger to know that we are loved; that our lives have meaning and purpose; that we can be forgiven and find grace; that we are not alone; that there is always hope. We hunger to know that even death will not be the end of us; and we hunger for joy, and peace, goodness, and grace.

In this life, we wrestle with the temptation to believe that if we just had enough bread we would be happy. Luke, in the sign of the manger, is reminding us that Jesus is the only one who can truly satisfy the hunger of our hearts.

Bread of Heaven, feed me till I want no more. Help me to trust in your love and to live in your grace. Help me to be a part of your purpose. Fill me with your Spirit, and guide me by your love. Amen.

26. The Visit of the Magi
Matthew 2:1-2

In the time of King Herod, after Jesus was born in Bethlehem of Judea, wise men from the East came to Jerusalem, asking, "Where is the child who has been born king of the Jews? For we observed his star at its rising, and have come to pay him homage."

LUKE TELLS US ABOUT THE SHEPHERDS and the manger. Matthew doesn't mention these at all. In fact, Matthew merely states that Jesus was born in Bethlehem. He then tells us that sometime after Jesus was born, "wise men from the East" came to pay him homage. By the time the wise men arrived, Mary and Jesus were staying in a home.

I invite you to review what I have written about the wise men in the companion book, *The Journey: Walking the Road to Bethlehem,* and what I mention there concerning King Herod the Great. Here I simply want to point out that the wise men were likely Zoroastrian priests from the area that today we call Iran. They were also likely astrologers, a profession which at that time was highly regarded, somewhere between modern-day astrology and astronomy.

God beckoned the wise men to make a several-month journey to see the infant Jesus, even though these men were likely not Jews. What does this tell you about God's concern and interest in the nations of the earth, not simply in the Jews? In some ways this story reminds me of the story of Jonah, the reluctant prophet whom God used to call the Assyrian people to repentance.

When the wise men found Mary and Jesus they were "overwhelmed with joy." They then presented gifts they had brought all the way from Persia—gifts of gold, frankincense, and myrrh.

You may know that these gifts were signs pointing toward Jesus' future identity. Gold is the gift of kings, and Jesus was the "King of kings." Frankincense was used by priests in their offerings to God, pointing toward Jesus' role as our "high priest." And myrrh was used in embalming the dead, a gift that pointed, even then, to the fact that Jesus would one day die. The Christmas gifts of the magi also likely sustained Joseph, Mary, and Jesus when they fled to Egypt, becoming refugees there, after learning that Herod wanted to kill Jesus.

Our congregation's offerings on Christmas Eve are one way of identifying with the magi in worship and of helping children in poverty. I've mentioned earlier in this book that on Christmas Eve night, our congregation gives away its entire offering, half to causes in a developing nation (currently, Malawi, Africa) and the other half to initiatives for children in poverty in Kansas City. This practice has proven to be very compelling not only for our members, but for the many visitors at Christmas Eve services. Last year a young man came to me after worship and said, "I'm a Buddhist, and my friends invited me to come tonight. I loved the music and your message, but what most moved me was the fact that your congregation voted to give away the entire offering tonight for children in poverty. I'll be back!"

Christmas has become, for most Americans, a season for gluttonous and overindulgent excess. But the wise men model for us a different approach to Christmas. They were not seeking to get more, but to give what they had to help the child and his family. Today we give what we have to help others in Christ's family.

In recent years, a younger generation has sometimes accused Christians of judgmentalism, hypocrisy, and insensitivity to the needs of others.[1] Yet this same generation is drawn to people and causes who, in the words of Micah, "do justice, and love mercy, and walk humbly with God."[2] It may well be that when our celebration of Jesus' birth begins to mirror the magi's celebration, then a younger generation will begin to see the power of the Christian faith.

For more information about how you or your church can give as the magi did, or for possible projects to consider, go to www.JourneyThisChristmas.com.

Lord, help me to look for ways, in my sphere of influence and in my daily life, that I can "do justice, and love kindness, and walk humbly" with you. Grant me a generous heart. Amen.

---

1. See David Kinnaman and Gabe Lyons' book, *UnChristian: What a New Generation Really Thinks About Christianity* (Baker Books, 2007).
2. See Micah 6:8.

27. The Light of the World
John 1:1-5

In the beginning was the Word, and the Word was with God, and the Word was God. He was in the beginning with God. All things came into being through him, and without him not one thing came into being. What has come into being in him was life, and the life was the light of all people. The light shines in the darkness, and the darkness did not overcome it.

NO ONE KNOWS WHEN JESUS WAS BORN. December 25 was chosen not because someone had a copy of Jesus' birth certificate, but because, as the early church pondered when to celebrate Jesus' birth, the winter solstice seemed the perfect time.[1] They chose this time, I believe, not because it was already a pagan festival, though it was. I believe they chose this date because on this night the heavens themselves seemed to tell the Christmas story.

At the winter solstice, the world seems to change. Up to that day, the nights have been growing longer and the days shorter. Darkness has been defeating the light. But after the winter solstice, the days grow longer and the night grows shorter. Light overcomes darkness.

We have focused in this book on Matthew and Luke's telling of the Christmas story; but John, too, tells the story of Christmas. He does not include shepherds or angels or wise men. He tells the story thus: "In the beginning was the Word, and the Word was with God and the Word was God. . . . What has come into being in him was life, and the life was the light of all people. The light shines in the darkness, and the darkness did not over-come it." When better to celebrate the one who himself was light, who defeated the darkness, than on the winter solstice!

We observe candlelight services at Christmas in part to commemorate the triumph of light over darkness that happens through Jesus Christ. The candlelighting portion of the service begins by extinguishing all the candles and turning out the lights in our sanctuary. We stand in the darkness, recalling the moments in our lives and in our world when darkness has seemed palpable. You can't appreciate the light of Christ that comes to us at Christmas until you've first felt and known the darkness. Finally in our candlelight service, we bring in one candle from the back of the room—the Christ candle—representing Jesus himself. We then begin to pass the candlelight throughout the room, lighting one another's candles as we sing "Silent Night."

When we finish passing the light, we invite everyone to hold their candles high in the air, and we all just look around. The room that was pitch dark a few minutes before is now filled with the soft glow of candlelight. And this, we note, is the point of Christmas—God came to us in Jesus Christ to dispel the darkness with his light. Hate, violence, bigotry, war, poverty, disease, sin, and even death seem so often to rule the world. But Jesus came to show us that God is, that God loves, and that hate and evil will not ultimately prevail.

I remind the congregation as we stand holding our candlelight that at one point in his ministry Jesus said, "I am the light of the world!" But as he called his disciples and invited them to follow, he said to them, "You are the light of the world. A city built on a hill cannot be hid. No one after lighting a lamp puts it under the bushel basket, but on the lampstand, and it gives light to all in the house. In the same way, let your light shine before others, so that they may see your good works and give glory to your Father in heaven" (Matthew 5:14-16). In this moment we see that Christmas is not only a gift from God—light piercing our darkness—it is also a calling from God to take his light into the world by our acts of love, mercy, and justice.

I'll offer just one small example of the simple ways this mission is lived out: A couple of years ago on Christmas Eve, Karla, our pastor to senior adults, went to a nearby nursing home and went room to room, offering to read the Christmas story from the Gospels. After reading, she prayed with the residents and then moved on to the next room. She came to a room that was dark; the lights were off and the shades were drawn. She hesitated to go in but then noticed a woman sitting on the edge of the bed in the darkness, her hands folded in her lap, as though she were waiting for someone or something.

Karla asked if she could come in and read the Christmas story, and the woman whispered, "Yes." After reading about the birth of Jesus, Karla prayed with the woman and then invited her to join in the Lord's Prayer.

Karla wished her a Merry Christmas and slipped out of the room. As she left, Karla heard the woman weeping quietly. She turned and stood at the door for a moment and heard the woman praying, "Lord, you didn't forget me. I prayed that you wouldn't forget me, and you didn't." Karla went back into the room, wrapped her arms around the woman, and held her as she wept. There in the darkness, light had come. It came because Christ was born in Bethlehem. It came because Karla had seen the light and felt compelled to share the light.

Christmas is God's gift to us, a gift of light and life, hope and grace. The gift is a reflection of God's concern for the world, and God's desire to heal it and drive away its darkness. The gift of Christmas therefore comes with a mission, a calling, and a responsibility. We must bear Christ's light into the world by our love, expressed through works of mercy and justice. At Christmas we are invited to receive Christ's light, but not only to receive it.

We are invited to bear the light, to walk in the light, and to take the light into the world.

Lord, I accept your light, your love, your mercy, and your grace. Fill me with your love. By your Holy Spirit help me to reflect your light, to walk in your light, and to take your light into the world. Amen.

---

1. Under the old Julian calendar the winter solstice was set as December 25. The Gregorian calendar we now use has the winter solstice occurring in the Northern Hemisphere on December 21/22, but this calendar was not adopted until the 1500s.

28. The Christmas Story in Matthew and Luke

On Christmas morning in my home, before we open our gifts, we light a candle, symbolic of Christ's presence and the light he brings to the world. Then we read the Christmas story as found in Matthew and Luke, and then we pray. It seems appropriate to end these reflections in the same way. I invite you to read the Christmas story as you celebrate on Christmas morning this year.

The Christmas Story in the Gospel of Matthew

NOW THE BIRTH OF JESUS THE MESSIAH took place in this way. When his mother Mary had been engaged to Joseph, but before they lived together, she was found to be with child from the Holy Spirit. Her husband Joseph, being a righteous man and unwilling to expose her to public disgrace, planned to dismiss her quietly. But just when he had resolved to do this, an angel of the Lord appeared to him in a dream and said, "Joseph, son of David, do not be afraid to take Mary as your wife, for the child conceived in her is from the Holy Spirit. She will bear a son, and you are to name him Jesus, for he will save his people from their sins." All this took place to fulfill what had been spoken by the Lord through the prophet:

"Look, the virgin shall conceive and bear a son,
and they shall name him Emmanuel,"

which means, "God is with us." When Joseph awoke from sleep, he did as the angel of the Lord commanded him; he took her as his wife, but had no marital relations with her until she had borne a son; and he named him Jesus.

—Matthew 1:18-25

The Christmas Story in the Gospel of Luke

I<small>N THOSE DAYS</small> a decree went out from Emperor Augustus that all the world should be registered. This was the first registration and was taken while Quirinius was governor of Syria. All went to their own towns to be registered. Joseph also went from the town of Nazareth in Galilee to Judea, to the city of David called Bethlehem, because he was descended from the house and family of David. He went to be registered with Mary, to whom he was engaged and who was expecting a child. While they were there, the time came for her to deliver her child. And she gave birth to her firstborn son and wrapped him in bands of cloth, and laid him in a manger, because there was no place for them in the inn.

In that region there were shepherds living in the fields, keeping watch over their flock by night. Then an angel of the Lord stood before them, and the glory of the Lord shone around them, and they were terrified. But the angel said to them, "Do not be afraid; for see—I am bringing you good news of great joy for all the people: to you is born this day in the city of David a Savior, who is the Messiah, the Lord. This will be a sign for you: you will find a child wrapped in bands of cloth and lying in a manger." And suddenly there was with the angel a multitude of the heavenly host, praising God and saying,

"Glory to God in the highest heaven,
    and on earth peace among those whom he favors!"

When the angels had left them and gone into heaven, the shepherds said to one another, "Let us go now to Bethlehem and see this thing that has taken place, which the Lord has made known to us." So they went with haste and found Mary and Joseph, and the child lying in the manger. When they saw this, they made known what had been told them about this child; and all who heard it were amazed at what the shepherds told them. But Mary treasured all these words and pondered them in her heart. The shepherds returned, glorifying and praising God for all they had heard and seen, as it had been told them.

—Luke 2:1-20

Lord, thank you for coming to us in Jesus Christ. Thank you for the salvation he brings. Thank you for your love, mercy, and grace. Thank you for Christmas. Help us to live as Christ-followers and to take your light into the world. Amen.

A New Christmas Tradition

On Christmas Eve, we invite our congregation to give of
what is precious to them as an expression of their joy and
gratitude for the birth of Jesus and his role in their lives.
For some who are struggling financially, the gift may be
something small, but all are invited to give something if they
are able. These gifts are then given to projects benefiting
children in poverty, divided equally between projects in the
developing world (currently Africa) and in our own inner
city. This has become one of our most meaningful traditions.
Even those who are nonreligious find this to be a moving
part of the service.

Mike Slaughter, pastor of the Ginghamsburg United
Methodist Church, reminds his congregation each year that
"Christmas is not your birthday!" Consider giving a special
offering this Christmas, for people in need. If you have children, teach your children this tradition, and help them learn
that Christmas is not primarily about what is under the tree,
but about God's gift of Jesus Christ, and, in turn, Christ's
call upon our lives to give ourselves for others.

If you found *The Journey* meaningful,

consider reading its companion,

24 Hours That Changed the World,

a moving study of the final hours of Jesus' life,

from the Last Supper to his crucifixion.

———————————————

Learn more about Adam Hamilton

and his ministry at

www.JourneyThisChristmas.com